A NOTE TO PARENTS

With this book you have an opportunity to introduce children to the Ten Commandments. It is important for young children to see these commandments as God's guides for living together happily, rather than a fearful set of laws. These rules for living have served us well for thousands of years.

The story of receiving the commandments is told briefly in concrete terms for young children. Because children cannot understand the abstract concept of idolatry, we have intentionally left out the story of worshiping the golden calf.

Since the rules are primarily adult concepts, you will find it helpful to use the paraphrase on the last pages of this book. Affirm actions in the child that carry out these rules, saying, "You are using God's rules, and that helps us to live together happily!"

– Delia Halverson

Delia Halverson is the consultant for *Family Time Bible Stories.* An interdenominational lecturer on religious education, she has written seven books, including *How Do Our Children Grow?*

Scripture sources: **Exodus 19-33**

FAMILY TIME
BIBLE
STORIES

THE TEN
COMMANDMENTS

Retold by Patricia Daniels

Illustrated by Troy Howell

ALEXANDRIA, VIRGINIA

Moses was a very old man, and his feet hurt. He was tired of walking on the hot, hard floor of the desert. He was weary of the glare of the sun. And the families following him were weary, too. They had been walking for months, looking for the promised land.

Moses had rescued the people of Israel from a cruel life in Egypt. Now they were looking for a new home.

Grandmothers, fathers, long-legged children, and babies on their mothers' backs followed him. Even sheep and camels trotted along the dry, rocky paths.

Sometimes the people were scared. Sometimes
they were lonely in the silent desert night.

But they knew that God spoke to Moses. They knew
that God and Moses would take care of them.

Finally they reached the foot of tall, bar-
ren mountains. Moses stopped. "Let us
make our camp here and rest," he said.
The people set up tents. They put their
babies down on soft blankets. Children
fed donkeys and told stories to each
other in the long shadows of evening.

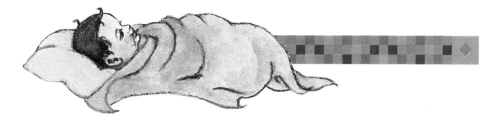

That night, Moses knelt down and
prayed to God. God said to Moses, "In
three days I will come down to this
mountain in a thick cloud. The people
will hear me speak to you there, but
tell them not to come too close."

Moses told his people to get ready. On the third day, storm clouds wrapped the mountaintop. Thunder shook the ground. The people of Israel trembled in fear. But Moses took his walking stick and climbed up the steep sides of the mountain, into the storm itself.

Moses pushed himself up, step by step, through the wind and thunder. He was calm. He knew that God loved him and his people. God must have something very important to tell them, he thought. When he reached the top of the mountain, he stopped and waited for God's voice. And then God spoke:

"I am the Lord, your God, who brought you out of Egypt," said God. "These are the rules that all my people should obey."

God told Moses that people should honor and respect their families. No one should lie or steal. God gave Moses the ten rules that people today call the Ten Commandments.

Many days passed while Moses spoke to God on the mountaintop. The people on the ground began to worry. All they could see on the mountain was a tumbling, flashing storm. God seemed to speak with the voice of thunder.

"Where is Moses?" they began to ask each other. "Will we be lost in this desert without him?"

But then, walking slowly out of the storm, Moses appeared. He was carrying something heavy in each arm.

What was Moses carrying? Great smooth stones—and on them were written the Ten Commandments, carved into the rock by God.

And Moses brought not just rules, but a promise. "God will lead us to the promised land," he said. "There we will find milk and honey. There we will make our homes."

In time, this promise was kept. The people of Israel reached the beautiful land of Canaan. They brought the commandments with them, in a carved golden box, to their new home. In this hopeful place, they would try to live by God's rules forever.

The Ten Commandments

Worship only God.

Do not worship a statue or a picture as God.

Do not use God's name except with respect.

Keep the seventh day of the week as a day of rest.

Honor your father and mother.

Do not kill.

Love your husband or wife.

Do not steal.

Do not tell lies about other people.

Do not be jealous of other people's belongings.

TIME-LIFE KIDS™
Staff for FAMILY TIME BIBLE STORIES

Managing Editor:	Patricia Daniels
Art Director:	Susan K. White
Publishing Associate:	Marike van der Veen
Editorial Assistant:	Mary M. Saxton
Copy Editor:	Colette Stockum
Production Manager:	Marlene Zack
Quality Assurance Manager:	Miriam Newton

First printing. Printed in U.S.A.   Published simultaneously in Canada.

Time Life Inc. is a wholly owned subsidiary of THE TIME INC. BOOK COMPANY.

TIME-LIFE is a trademark of Time Warner Inc. U.S.A.
School and library distribution by Time-Life Education,
P.O. Box 85026, Richmond, VA 23285-5026.
For subscription information, call 1-800-621-7026.

Library of Congress Cataloging-in-Publication Data

Daniels, Patricia, 1955-   The ten commandments/ retold by Patricia Daniels; illustrated by Troy Howell. p. cm.—(Family time Bible stories) Summary: Tells how Moses led the Israelites out of Egypt to the land promised them by God and how he brought them God's commandments.
ISBN 0-7835-4631-9 1. Ten commandments—Juvenile literature. 2. Bible stories, English—O.T. Exodus. 3. Bible stories, English—O.T. Deuteronomy. [1. Moses (Biblical leader) 2. Exodus, The. 3. Ten commandments. 4. Bible stories—O.T.]. I. Howell, Troy, ill. II. Title. III. Series.
BS1285.5.D26 1996   96-15330
222'.1609505— dc20   CIP
                                          AC